# The Art of Decorative Paper Stencils

# THE ART OF DECORATIVE PAPER STENCILS

KANAKO YAGUCHI

QUARRY BOOKS

First published in 2007 in Japan by
Ikeda Shoten Publishing Co. Ltd.,
43 Benten-cho, Shinjuku-ku, Tokyo 162-0851, Japan
www.ikedashoten.co.jp
under the title of *Yasashii Kirigami*

First published in 2008 in the United States of America by
Quarry Books, a member of
Quayside Publishing Group
100 Cummings Center / 406-L
Beverly, Massachusetts 01915
USA
Phone: 978-282-9590
FAX: 978-283-2742
www.rockpub.com

English translation rights arranged with
Ikeda Shoten Publishing co., LTD
through Rico Komanoya, ricorico, Tokyo, Japan.

Translation: Seishi Maruyama
Copy-editing: Alma Reyes-Umemoto
Editing: Omegasha Co., Ltd.
Art direction: Takuji Segawa (Killigraph)
Book Design: Eiko Nishida (cooltiger, ltd.) and
Andrew Pothecary (forbiddencolour)
Photographs: Watanabe (Photos in studio, 3-D works,
author's recent photo) and Tomohiro Akasaka (Paper
stencils, instructions for 3-D works)
Illustrations: Kiyoshi Matsui
Interview and photo collaboration: pour annick Harajuku
(furniture: desk, desk chair, round table, and vase on
pages 78-79) and studio school
Production: Aki Ueda (ricorico)
Chief editor and producer: Rico Komanoya (ricorico)

ISBN-13: 978-1-59253-440-1
ISBN-10: 1-59253-440-6

10 9 8 7 6 5 4 3 2 1

Printed in China by Everbest Printing Co., Ltd.

# Contents

## Creative Objects with Decorative Paper Stencils  78

# A Paper Stencils Travelogue

I always carried a pair of scissors and some paper with me when I was a child. I thought that I could use these tools to transmit my thoughts directly into visual expressions, then send them to someone afar. I have always felt that paper stencils and travels are connected. Today, whenever I go out, I still carry a pair of scissors with me, and I create something with a piece of paper I find by chance in any of my travels. Unpredictable events during my travels provide me useful images and hints for creating paper stencils. I remember feeling the air and the temperature outside the airport and seeing the sky and the city in distinctive colors. Memories of delicious food in restaurants and the strange smell of galleries and museums remain in my mind. These memories do not fade over time, and I recall them clearly in my paper stencil work. Various colors and characteristic shapes reflect each country or location much in the same way that paper stencils can have a wide range of colors and shapes. This book features a collection of paper stencil works, which I have created during my travels. Join me in this travelogue about my world of paper stencils.

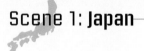

## Scene 1: Japan

I unexpectedly found a gift from the past inside my drawer that I could not give away. At that moment I saw subtle reflections of a garden cast on the shoji paper screen in my room through the soft light from the outside. This scene brought back the good, old days of Japanese scenes that I had almost forgotten.

# Scene 2: China

I recall what I saw and felt in
China, the country of whirling
energy—the sun setting
on the vast motherland
and people crowded in
squares and streets.
One feels the dynamic rhythm
of motion and stillness of
daily life. I want to express
the landscape where two
extreme aspects—delicacy
and boldness or past and
present moments—coexist.

## Scene 3: Thailand

I find an Asian mystery hidden in the color of lotus flowers, which give off a slight fragrance through the transparent air. The people's traditional thoughts are well preserved and they appear through symbolic figures in the changing times. The sun always rises high up in the sky and shines on various ethnic objects.

# Scene 4: France

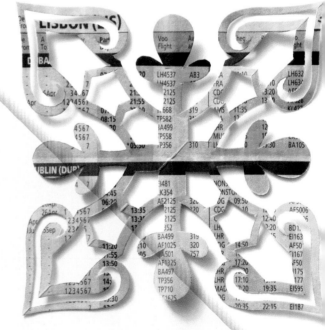

While I traveled by train in France I found the secret keys to the treasure boxes hidden in the various towns. As soon as I opened the boxes, everything before me began to sparkle brilliantly. The keys locked tokens beyond the ages, and were passed on carefully from one person to another, making me feel the dignity and warmth of their significance.

## Scene 5: Portugal

A pleasant breeze passes through casual conversations and events, a tram jolts slowly along the street, and the birds fly away elegantly over the hills that reveal a streamline. I want to express the honesty and kindness I have learned in this country, which spread over its ordinary landscape.

# Scene 6: USA

I found a picture in a workshop. Office workers walked, and I gazed at the building and the artwork. There is always something that never changes amidst the different lives of various races. As I got off at the same station and turned the same corner of the street I used to walk on, I arrived at the same place.

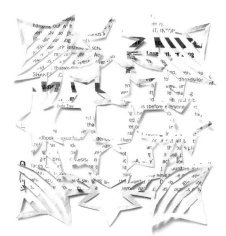

# Preparing for Your Travels with Paper Stencils
## Basic Guide to Paper-Stencil Making

Passport, ticket, camera, my favorite clothes and shoes... I always get excited when packing, and I feel the same way when preparing for my travel with paper stencils. Before we depart, however, we need to know the basic guide to paper-stencil making.

You can create decorative paper stencils in three easy steps: fold, cut, and open. Position the paper as indicated in the section for folding on page 31, and then cut out the design, leaving the colored area behind. If you find it difficult to cut out the design directly by just looking at the pattern, you can trace the design onto the paper before cutting.

# Basic Guide to Paper-Stencil Making
## 1 Basic Tools

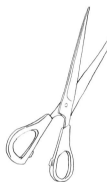

### Scissors
One of the necessary tools that you need to prepare for paper-stencil making is a pair of sharp scissors. Select one that fits comfortably in your hand.

### Paper (origami paper)
You can use any type of colored paper, but origami paper is preferable and is readily available anywhere.

### Glue
You need glue to stick your finished work on a sketchbook. You can use a glue stick, spray glue, or liquid glue depending on the type of paper you use.

### Sketchbook
You can keep origami paper, business cards, and newspapers you have collected on your trips, and many other types of paper in a sketchbook. This will serve as your travel book.

# 2 How Paper Stencils Work

Paper stencils are very simple to create. They require only a pair of scissors and a sheet of paper. You don't have to limit yourself to origami paper; wrapping paper and newspaper can also be used. Then, just fold, cut, and open. With these three actions, you will be able to create lovely paper stencil artwork.

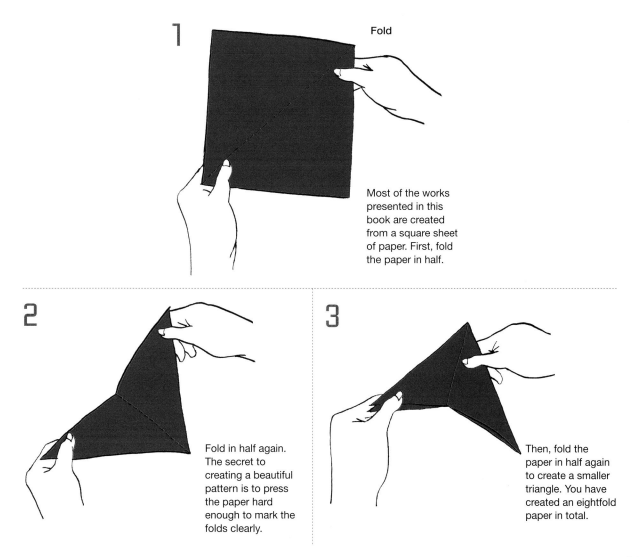

**1** Fold

Most of the works presented in this book are created from a square sheet of paper. First, fold the paper in half.

**2**

Fold in half again. The secret to creating a beautiful pattern is to press the paper hard enough to mark the folds clearly.

**3**

Then, fold the paper in half again to create a smaller triangle. You have created an eightfold paper in total.

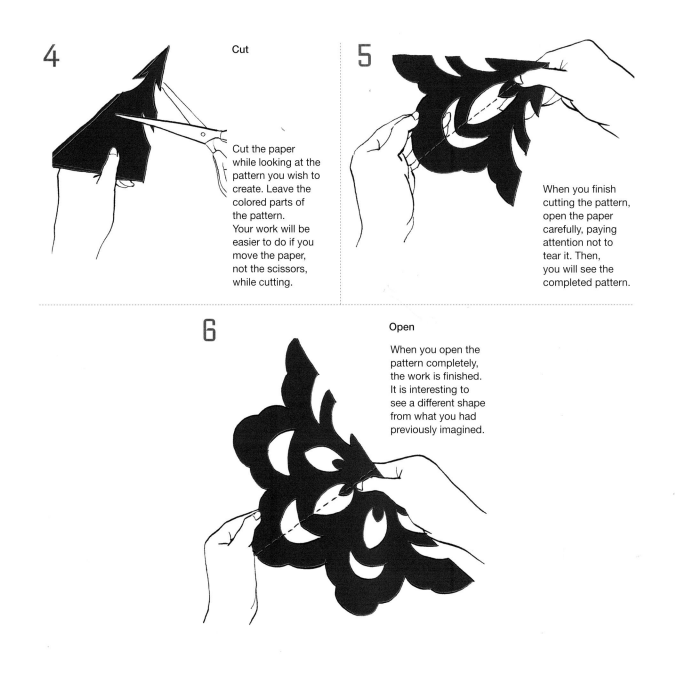

**4** Cut

Cut the paper
while looking at the
pattern you wish to
create. Leave the
colored parts of
the pattern.
Your work will be
easier to do if you
move the paper,
not the scissors,
while cutting.

**5**

When you finish
cutting the pattern,
open the paper
carefully, paying
attention not to
tear it. Then,
you will see the
completed pattern.

**6** Open

When you open the
pattern completely,
the work is finished.
It is interesting to
see a different shape
from what you had
previously imagined.

# 3 Folding Methods

First, fold the paper simply before cutting it. The paper stencils presented in this book can be created by folding the paper into two shapes: triangle and rectangle.

## Making a Triangle (Variation)

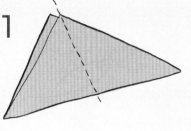

1

The triangle variation presented here folds the paper into a triangle, but in a different way. First, fold a square sheet of paper in half. Then, fold in half again to mark the fold.

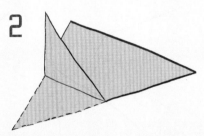

2

Fold diagonally toward the fold marked in the center.

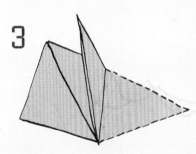

3

Fold the other side in the same way toward the center.

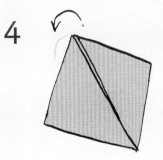

4

Fold the paper in half inward to the center to make a triangle.

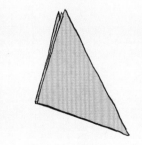

5

This is the completed triangle. The layers of the paper should not come out so that the triangle is stable when you cut a pattern.

## Making a Rectangle

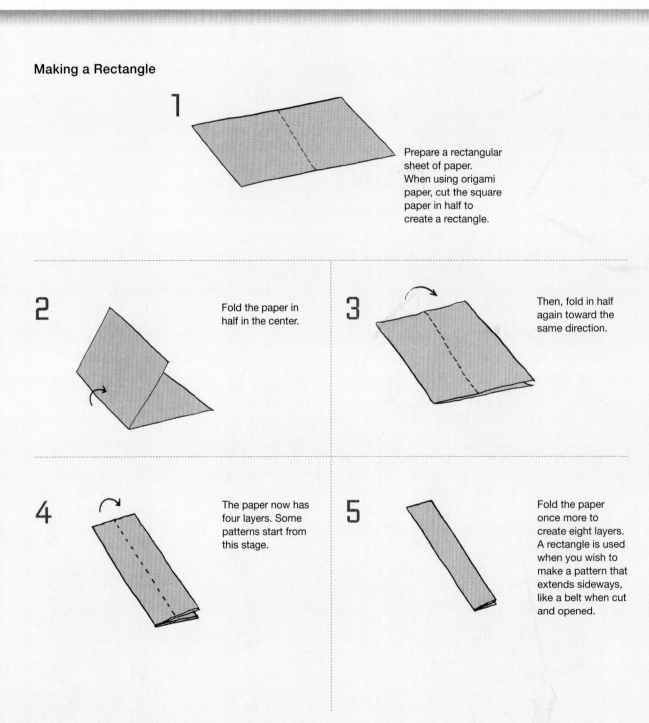

**1**

Prepare a rectangular sheet of paper. When using origami paper, cut the square paper in half to create a rectangle.

**2** Fold the paper in half in the center.

**3** Then, fold in half again toward the same direction.

**4** The paper now has four layers. Some patterns start from this stage.

**5** Fold the paper once more to create eight layers. A rectangle is used when you wish to make a pattern that extends sideways, like a belt when cut and opened.

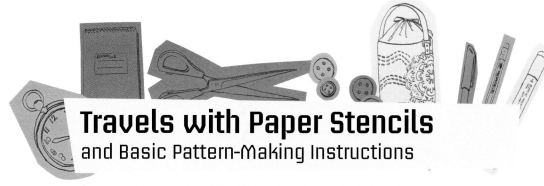

# Travels with Paper Stencils
## and Basic Pattern-Making Instructions

Once you have mastered the fold, cut, and open technique for paper-stencil making, you can create the patterns introduced in this chapter. However, these designs are only for reference. You may find your own unique way of making decorative paper stencils.

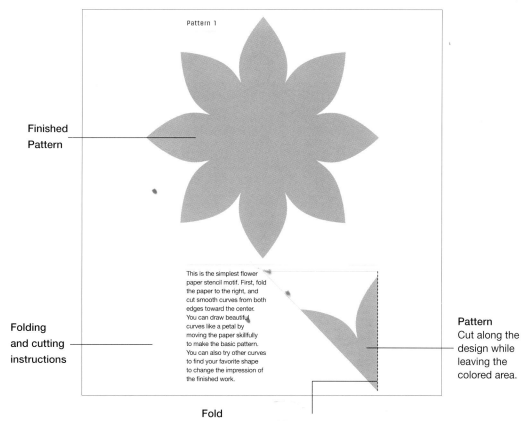

Pattern 1

**Finished Pattern**

**Folding and cutting instructions**

This is the simplest flower paper stencil motif. First, fold the paper to the right, and cut smooth curves from both edges toward the center. You can draw beautiful curves like a petal by moving the paper skillfully to make the basic pattern. You can also try other curves to find your favorite shape to change the impression of the finished work.

**Pattern**
Cut along the design while leaving the colored area.

**Fold**
After making a triangle or a rectangle, position the fold as indicated in the pattern before cutting with scissors. The fold is indicated by a dotted line.

# Japan

The delicate light, refreshing air, landscape, climate, and language of every place are slightly different from each other. Yet, there is a common sensation that we feel in each place that penetrates our bodies naturally. The modest, vigorous, and beautiful flowers are in full bloom, which reflect images of Japan. The decorative paper stencils will make you feel the flowers of the changing seasons.

## Memories of My Trip

At the end of the tourist season, my family often went for a trip. My father drove our car; my mother made rice balls in a lunch box early in the morning; and my two sisters and I sat leaning against each other in the back seat of the car as we talked, ate, and sang. I wondered if it was because I felt secure inside the car that I slept for so long, and I remember seeing the vast, blue sky every time I woke up. These childhood memories have made me enjoy traveling and feeling the beauty of nature until today.

When I was twenty years old, I visited Kyoto and Nara again in the fall. I found new discoveries that were different from what I saw in my childhood. I witnessed a traditional and modest Japanese natural beauty, especially in keeping plants as parts of everyday life, and I thought that I had to respect these good aspects of Japanese life. Such thoughts are reflected in my decorative paper stencils. The memories of the places I visited in my childhood are fragmented, but when I revisit them in my adulthood, the experiences are revived. They remained asleep for a long time, but have now brought me a new breeze with the memories of the good, old days. This breeze will carry me further ahead.

Pattern 1  Pattern 2  Pattern 3  Pattern 4  Pattern 5  Pattern 6

# Instructions for Making Paper Stencils ⬤ Japan

Pattern 1

## Items of Inspiration

I like the colors and shapes of pottery, and I purchase different kinds to give me ideas for my creation. Thanks to them, my thoughts bring back inspiration for my work after a long journey.

This is the simplest flower paper-stencil motif. First, fold the paper to the right and cut smooth curves from both edges toward the center. You can draw beautiful curves like a petal by moving the paper skillfully to make the basic pattern. You can also try other curves to find your favorite shape and to change the impression of the finished work.

## Pattern 2

For this pattern, cut a natural curve at the base of the petals to make a perfect circle in the center.
As you have done for pattern 1, cut the paper into a petal shape from the edges toward the center.
To finish, hold the scissors at the inner edge of the center circle and cut out along it.

**Japan**

Pattern 3

Cut in straight slits from both ends of the paper toward the center of the flower. This part will form the shape of the central part of the pattern. The finished shape will change depending on whether the angle of the cut is sharp or obtuse. As done for pattern 2, cut off both sides and the outer portion as you form the shape of the petal.

## Pattern 4

This pattern is a variation of pattern 3 and differs in the cut of the tip of the petals. First, cut slits toward the center of the flower. Then, cut two more slits towards the outer part for the petal tips. Cut in a curve as you connect two slits in order to form the shape of a petal. If you make a deep curve, the petal will have a stronger image.

Pattern 5

This shape is accentuated
by the pattern in the tips.
It may appear difficult,
but it will be easier to work
on if you try not to cut a fine
pattern all at once.
Slowly and carefully combine
various cutting techniques.
Cut in slits, but leave two lines,
which correspond to the
tip of the petal.

## Pattern 6

To form the curve of the petal, cut in slits from both edges of the paper toward the center. If you cut the slits in the same length, the pattern will become uniformly symmetrical, but if you cut the slits in different lengths on the right and left sides, the image of the flower will be different. If you increase the number of slits, the petal pattern will appear more delicate and elegant.

# China

What I saw in China was beyond my imagination; my impression was more intense than I expected! It's like experiencing a dynamic power I have not seen in any other place.
I felt a contrasting element that sparked my sensitivity and overwhelmed me. My trip to China gave me strong impressions of the colors red and blue. If you visit China, I am sure you will find something you will never forget.

## Memories of My Trip

A trip always starts dramatically. Listening to the typhoon warning from the weather forecast, I nervously got on the plane to Beijing. Rain, wind, and thunder increased their intensity as the sky gradually became darker. The red lights from the plane and the lightning flashed alternately in the clouds. The three-hour flight felt ten times longer and made me feel that I had gone so far away. On the first night in Beijing, I felt some relief, calmness, and peace. The next morning, however, I woke up to an unexpectedly powerful city. It had vitality that seemed to renew anything. The old cityscape seemed to have vanished. But, in the old streets, you can see kids running around, grandmas knitting incredibly fast on a bench, and men gathering to have tea.

Next to this peaceful scene, you find massive historical buildings. I entered the palace from the front entrance, and after walking for three hours inside the building where the last emperor must have walked, a slightly elevated hill appeared. As I stood on top of the hill and gazed back at the view of the palace, with the street scenery around it, I felt the dignified strength from every detail of the city as reflected by the red sunset. The view of the palace buildings expanded below me as if they overlapped each other; it was so beautiful that I felt like it was my destiny to see the view at that exact moment of that day. This fantastic vision has been strongly impressed in my memory to this day.

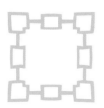

Pattern 1

Pattern 2

Pattern 3

Pattern 4

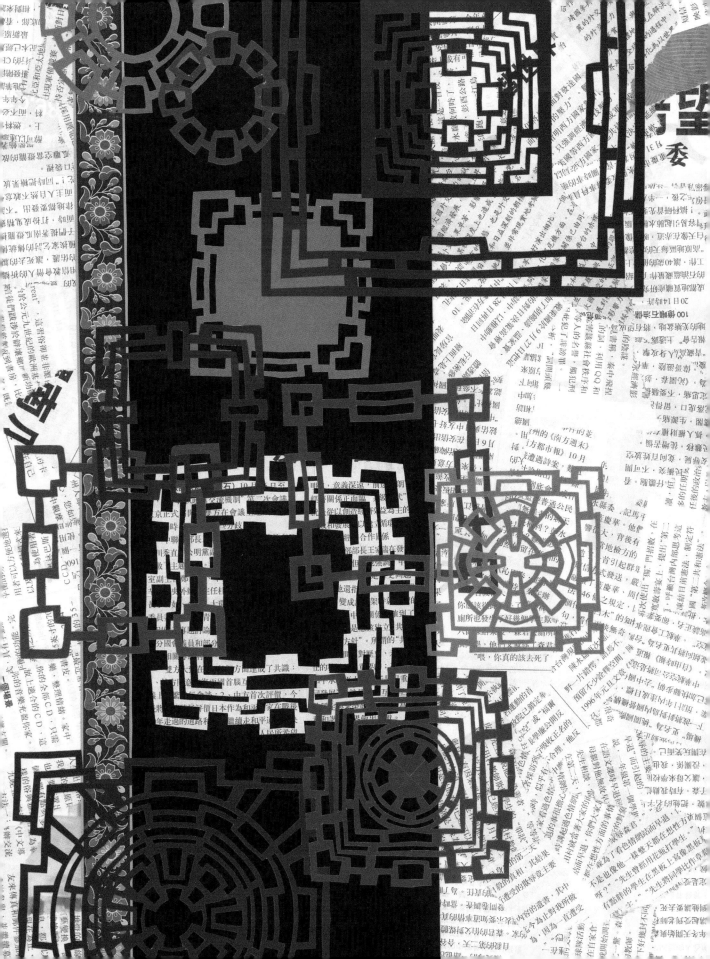

Pattern 1

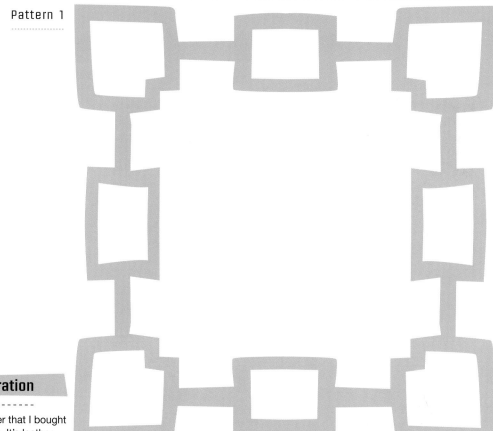

## **Items of Inspiration**

This is a small drawer that I bought at an antique market. It's leather-covered and the paper inside seems like old, pasted newspaper. There is a beautiful drawing on the surface that feels like a token from the creator.

As you visualize your image of China, make a pattern of squares connected to each other with lines. First, cut a square on both sides of the paper. Try to make the squares parallel to the upper edge of the paper. Finish by cutting the inner and outer parts of the squares on both sides. You can make a more precise square by cutting the paper in constant widths.

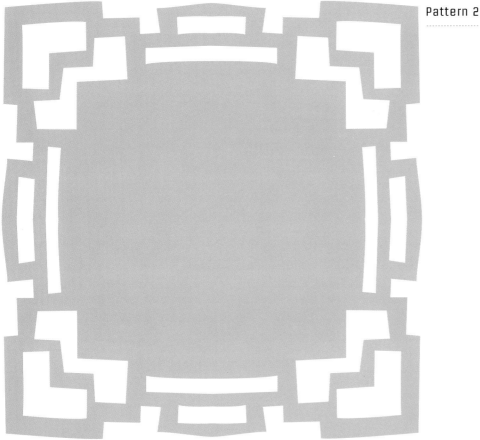

First, cut a narrow rectangle on the left side of the paper, then cut an "L" shape along the narrow rectangle. On the right side of the paper, cut two narrow rectangles, one large and the other small. Finally, cut the outer part along the uneven edge of the inner part carefully in constant widths. You can also cut the central part in the same shape as pattern 1.

Pattern 3

This pattern is more complex but the basic cutting method is the same as the previous patterns. Cut narrow rectangles and "L" shapes from both sides along the top side of the folded paper. The effect will turn out nicely if the slits are cut irregularly. You can also try cutting more slits to create your own original patterns.

## Pattern 4

This is a circular shape that can be added to the previous rectangular patterns. First, cut a circle in the center with a smooth curve. Cut a rectangle and "L" shapes along this curve. Then, cut a big square along the left side of the "L" shape and another square of the same size along the right side of the "L" shape. To finish, cut off the outer parts.

# Thailand

As I passed through a busy crowd, amidst the humidity, I found a mysterious landscape that evoked a strange sensation. I saw floating lotus flowers that swayed gently on the water and a huge, gold image of Buddha. As I looked at them all day long, I felt as though the stress on my shoulders started to disappear. These images are stored in my memory like a dream as I take my nap after lunch under a tree.

## Memories of My Trip

As soon as I arrived in Thailand, the unique smell and muggy, dull air passed through my body. That happened not too long after I started working on my decorative paper stencils. I didn't have the slightest idea what would happen next. My unplanned trip, which seemed to symbolize this uncertain period of my life, never seemed to happen.

After sitting on a bus traveling from Bangkok for over ten hours, I got on a boat and traveled for a few more hours. I finally arrived on an island that appeared so mysterious that I felt like it was a gift from God. The taste of watermelon in the middle of the night, the air at dawn while I waited for a boat, the forest stretching out under the bright sunshine, the Milky Way that shimmered on the dark ocean at night— I miss all these landscapes increasingly as my memory fades over time.

I met a Japanese man during that long bus trip. The lonely feeling of being the only Japanese people in that area eased as we exchanged information about our travels. Since we had different places of interest, he took a picture of us as a souvenir, then we separated without exchanging our addresses. A few years later, we met once again in Tokyo, thanks to the photograph he brought with him. Since that encounter, he has been one of my most important friends and undeniable teachers in my life. I wonder if it was the mystery of Thailand that made me connect to many other people after that reunion?

Pattern 1

Pattern 2

Pattern 3

Pattern 4

**Pattern 4**

First, cut the outer edge of the paper from both sides. Cut both sides with a gradual curve along the shape of the outer edge. Finally, cut a slit from one side along the two triangular shapes on both sides. In order to make the slit, made a deep cut, stop, then cut one more time. If the curve is natural, the center of the pattern should look like a four-leaf clover when you open it.

# France

Old churches and apartments; an old café; people in narrow alleys—I felt comfort in these everyday scenes, although I had come so far away from my ordinary life. What if I could turn scenes, such as the sunlight coming through the trees or the light blinking from the street lamps on a long night, into shapes?

## Memories of My Trip

While I traveled by train from Paris to Nice, I suddenly awoke in the middle of the night and looked out from the window to find out that there was no visible light anywhere except for thousands of stars in the sky. Each light blinked stronger and brighter than usual. I realized that the train had passed through many towns, and the landscape began to change gradually. Then, I felt as if I were under a spell of magic, as I wrote in my diary. As I read my notes again, I feel embarrassed to realize what a romantic trip it was, and slowly, but clearly the memories come back to me.

The roofs of the churches and the stained glass; the paintings and sculptures before my eyes; and the Eiffel Tower that stood eternally through the seasons never bored me. I am not a big fan of wine or oysters, but I miss the delicious duck. I also miss the snobbish waiters at the cafés, and the fabulous fashion.

As I continued my travel on my own pace, I got so tired that I fell asleep and slept through the night without dreaming until the next morning. I woke up earlier than usual, stretched, and opened the windows to breathe in the fresh air. I felt so refreshed in France no matter where I was that I could easily lose myself in creating paper stencils. But, then I look at my work in a thin, brand new light and I get a little bit excited about the future—what would be waiting for me today?

Pattern 1

Pattern 2

Pattern 3

Pattern 4

Pattern 1

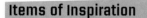

## **Items of Inspiration**

I procured some exotic-scented perfume and keys at the flea markets. These old keys must open doors of mysterious houses in the seductive city of Paris. Maybe they also open the doors to my world of decorative paper stencils?

This pattern takes the shape from an image of a cross in a church. First, cut the center of the sword's shape on the left side of the paper. The secret in producing a beautiful circle in the center of this pattern is to cut a slight curve in from the left edge. Next, cut along the sword's other edge. On the opposite side of the pattern, cut a smaller sword.

This pattern has a cross shape with round tips, resembling a flower bud. First, cut the shape of a large flower bud, and continue cutting toward the center. Turn the direction of the pattern, cutting backward to make a hornlike shape in the middle. Finally, cut a smaller flower bud with a smooth curve. You can change the size of each part if you'd like.

Pattern 3

This pattern takes the shape of a sword and a flower bud, combining patterns 1 and 2. First, cut the outline of a large flower bud, and cut a small sword shape from the opposite side of the paper. Cut a small triangle inside the sword, then cut the inner part of the flower bud, leaving a line in the middle. You can adjust this part as you like.

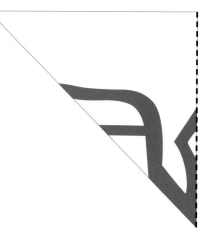

First, cut a curled slit and a platelike shape on the left side of the pattern. Then, cut a large flower bud shape from the outer part. Cut a shape carefully that sticks out in between the sword and the flower bud, and finally, make a small sword shape on the right side.

# Portugal

People laugh a lot, work hard, and enjoy delicious food in this country. I wanted to turn these scenes into shapes; for they gave me a sensation of a warm, soft breeze and a scent that loosens up people's minds.

I scurried along the streets with a map in my hand while entertaining these thoughts. I saw a city that shone brightly amidst the flow of the river and plenty of green. It's the only place where I felt my heart dance peacefully.

## Memories of My Trip

My trip to Portugal lasted only a few days; I felt like a backpacker. I got on the bus and tram with a map in my hand, and walked slowly up a hill. As I took a break at an open café, which had a great view, my tiredness blew away with the wind. My Coke tasted so great outdoors that moment, as I gazed at a peaceful city under the blue sky. I found a guest house and had a meal at a restaurant both by accident. I felt I could spend time for such mind-free travels without thinking or worrying too much about anything—just to loosen up my mind and relax naturally.

I traveled up to the north and stopped by the ocean. The sunlight flickered on the water. I became tired and hungry, and I decided to have an early dinner at a local restaurant. I watched an exciting soccer game on television with the local people and enjoyed my homemade meal, which I could only taste on such particular moments.

Time seems to pass by slowly in this city that I simply wanted to stop and look carefully at the trees swinging with the wind, or the boats floating calmly on the water. Somehow, I felt I could fit in this foreign land. The experience has taught me the simple reality that you can enjoy whatever pleases you and do whatever you desire—and you can restart your life over.

Pattern 1

Pattern 2

Pattern 3

Pattern 4

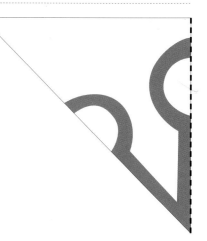

Pattern 1

## Items of Inspiration

These balls came in different shapes and sizes, hanging at a store window display or from the ceiling. They can be folded and opened into round shapes, which reminded me of decorative paper stencils.

This pattern of dynamic round shapes reflects my image of Portugal. This simple basic paper stencil consists of circles and straight lines. Cut a half circle on each side of the paper, then cut along the outer edge around the circles. You can create a different effect by adjusting the size of both circles or by changing the length or width of the lines that connect the circles.

This pattern has more circles than pattern 1, and the inner parts are not cut out. Cut one smaller circle that sticks out between the two circles on both sides of the paper. If you cut the stem of the circle with a small curve, you can produce an interesting effect: one that perhaps looks like a new bud that grows in the sunlight.

Pattern 3

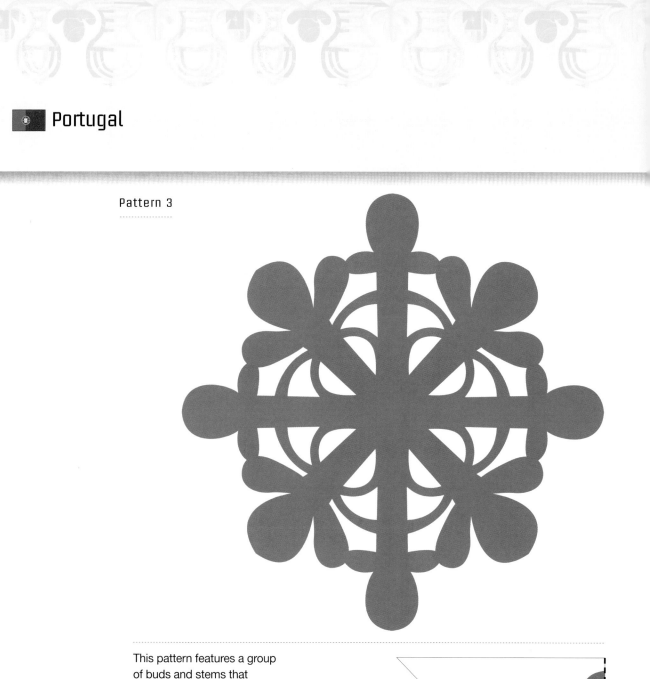

This pattern features a group of buds and stems that intertwine intricately. First, cut the image of buds (baby leaves) on the left side of the paper, then continue cutting down toward the center. From this point, cut the stem on the right side, moving upward very carefully. Finally, cut the images of the bud on the opposite side.

**TIP**
When working on patterns 3 and 4, it is better to make incisions first, as indicated by the arrows, before cutting in order not to let the pieces fall apart.

## Pattern 4

This pattern is taken from a rectangular piece of paper folded twice in the same direction (see page 34, Making a Rectangle, step 4). As with the shape of pattern 3, this pattern also depicts buds and stems intertwined together. The buds overlap at two points, but as you did for pattern 3, it is better to cut one side first before cutting the other side.

# USA

I always feel the same vibration in this country whenever I visit it, and I can always see the silhouette of the streets and the stars.

The outlines of different people from different walks of life project like a monochromatic photograph. I took a wider path and faster pace than usual, among the crowd of people that passed by busily. As I walked down the streets, it became clear to me that I was thinking too much.

## Memories of My Trip

I made my my first trip abroad during my freshman year in high school. At that time, everything was new to me and I found various scenes that I had seen in photographs. The colorful neon signs of New York City, excitement of the theaters, and the footsteps of anxious people entering the baseball stadium—those memories come back to me in fragments.

Among those memories, I have kept two unforgettable ones. One is when I got sick on my first day of the trip. I must have been nervous about the long two-month trip, or just worried whether I could go back to Japan safely.

The other one is when my trip was almost over. The slightly warm spring air eased my mind and made me forget myself while admiring the beautiful shoes displayed in the stores. My friend, with whom I traveled, got her bag stolen. Her passport, purse, diary, and camera were gone in a second. That type of accident remained as an important memory. In spite of it, we continued to visit the city almost every year, and we have fun memories to share. Now, I can explain which train station you should get off at, or which corner you should turn to get to certain places, while reflecting that the same fateful events we shared back then will never happen again—and those memories were important moments for me. I want to keep those moments in my heart and turn them into shapes.

Pattern 1

Pattern 2

Pattern 3

Pattern 4

Pattern 5

Pattern 6

Pattern 1

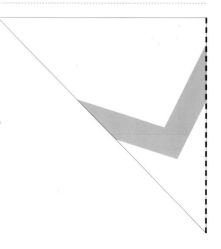

## Items of Inspiration

I can stay in museum shops, such as in the Museum of Modern Art (MOMA) and the Metropolitan Museum of Art, for hours without getting bored. I spend as much time shopping as I spend looking at artwork. The objects I purchase are also good reference materials for my creative work.

This pattern is that of a star. Cut the paper in a sharp angle from both sides toward the center. If you cut from the sides and meet at the middle point, the shape becomes a clear star. If you change the width and the angle, the shape will change. The cut in the center has a smaller star shape, so you can cut out many stars from one sheet of paper.

This shape looks like four stars holding hands. Cut the outer parts of the pattern from both sides. Leave the two parts that reach the right end uncut; they correspond to the connected parts of the tips of the stars when the pattern is opened. Try changing the angles and the sizes of the stars.

Pattern 3

Cut out shapes of a half star on both sides of the paper. It is important to cut two stars of the same size and to place the points of the star in the center. Cut off the inner and outer parts of the pattern along the shape of the cut-out stars to finish. When you open the pattern, a large star appears in the center. In order to produce a perfect-looking star, be careful to pay attention to the angle that you cut.

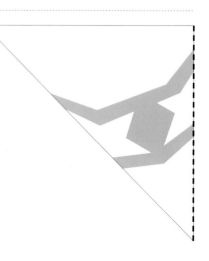

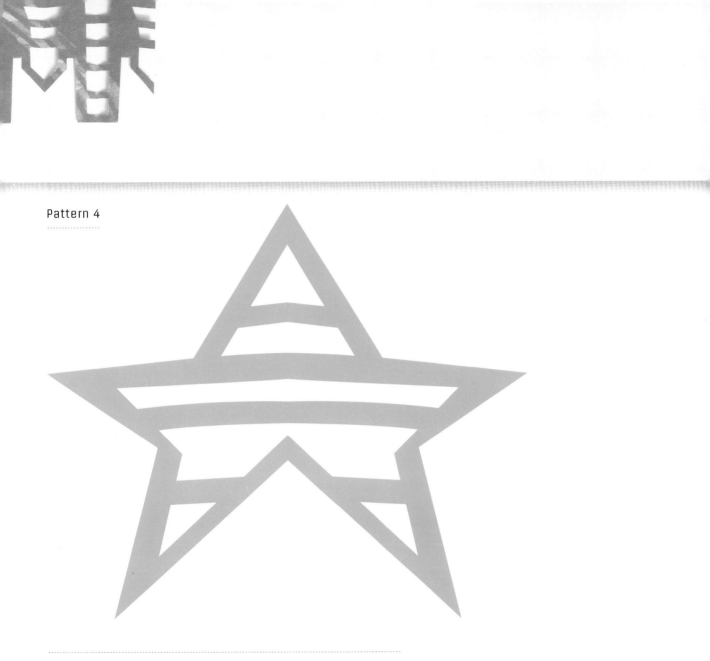

## Pattern 4

This pattern features horizontal stripes inside a star. Fold the paper in half. Place the fold on your right side and cut out the shape of a half star on the left side. Then, cut out stripes from the right side carefully so as not to cut off the outer frame. In order to cut out a triangle on the bottom, slash one part of the lowest stripe, as indicated by the red arrow.

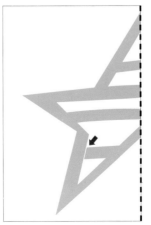

Pattern 5

This pattern features an image of New York City buildings. First, fold a rectangular piece of paper three times in the same direction (see page 34, Making a Rectangle, step 5). Place the fold on your right side and cut out an image of a building with a steep roof. Cut a rectangle for the windows of the buildings for the other side of the pattern. It's easier to cut if you imagine the silhouette of the building.

## Pattern 6

Use the same paper in pattern 5 that was folded three times in the same direction. Place the fold on your left side this time and cut out a few rectangles. Cut a shape of a roof for the right side of the pattern, then cut the outer portion of the building. You can change the size of the windows and the angle of the roof, or increase the number of square windows to add variety to the building's silhouettes.

# Creative Objects
## with Decorative Paper Stencils

When I come back home from a trip, the first thing I do is to relax and drink tea. After taking a break, I unpack my bags, which is the last fun part of my trip. I throw my clothes in the washing machine and I organize my souvenirs to give to my friends. Then, I have my pictures developed and finally, the best moment comes. I pull out the pieces of paper and tickets I gathered from different parts of the world, and open them like a piece of wrapping paper. I want to cut out my important memories and not confine them in photographs. Let's decorate our rooms with a lot of memories.

# Tea Mat

Before placing your tea cup on the table, lighten up your tea conversation with a beautiful tea mat.

## Materials
Paper stencil patterns
Cardboard
Thin sheet of paper
Stencil sheets
Stencil brushes
Paint
Transparent adhesive tape
Pencil
Cutting knife
Cutting mat

1

Paste a paper stencil pattern including its outer frame on a stencil sheet to make the tea mat pattern.

2

Turn the paper upside down to keep the pattern facing up, then cut along the paper stencil with a cutting knife.

3

Place the pattern in step 2 on a sheet of cardboard, then paint over it by tapping it lightly with a brush. If you apply several colors and overlap them, your artistic expression will be enhanced.

4

Place a larger paper stencil pattern on the rear side of the cardboard that you painted in step 3, and trace the shape with a pencil.

5

Cut the cardboard along the pencil line to finish. You can achieve a beautiful result if you paste a thin sheet of paper over the work.

6

You can change the cutting style to create other objects, such as a table mat, napkin holder, coaster, and more.

# Flower Vase Cover

Place your favorite flower in a vase and wrap it with your beautiful memories.

## Materials

Paper stencil works

Plastic sheet (measured to
  the size of the vase)

Colored paper (same size
  as the plastic sheet)

Spray glue

Cutting knife

Cutting mat

1  Attach your stencil work lightly on the plastic sheet with removable spray glue.

2  Cut out some patterns with a cutting knife. Then, remove the stencil.

3  Create slits of the same intervals, $1/2$ in (1.3 cm), in order to fit both ends of the board. It is easier to adjust the design if you put both ends of the paper together when cutting.

4 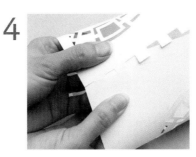 Fit both edges of the paper together and bend the slits when inserting them. Place the colored paper inside to finish.

# Souvenir Box

It's exciting to open a
souvenir from a box
that you created.

**Materials**

Paper stencil works

Box

Thin paper

Starch glue

Spray glue

Water

## Steps

1

Tear the thin paper into small pieces and attach them on an empty box.

2

Lay the paper stencil works on the box. Then, attach the thin paper with water-diluted starch glue over it.

3

Some of the stencil works can be attached with a strong spray glue on a piece of pink paper.

4

The colors of the stencils are quite noticeable, so arrange the layout to balance the total of color used.

# Book Cover

I can't spend a
day without books
during my travels.

**Materials**
Paper stencil works
Cloth; sample size:
   7.1 in x 13.8 in (18 cm
   x 35 cm)
Stencil sheets
Stencil brushes
Paints for fabric
Sewing machine
Craft knife
Cutting mat

1

Make a pattern with a stencil sheet (see pages 80-81), and paint designs on the cloth with paints for fabric.

2

Prepare a piece of cloth of the same size to be used for the reverse side of the stencil pattern.

3

Place the two sheets of cloth face to face and make a long tube. Fold both ends three times, then sew them to make a pocket for inserting the book cover.

4

Turn the cloth inside out so that the right side comes outside, and sew up the center, upper side, and lower side with a sewing machine. Hold the central part with marking pins.

# Photo Frame

These frames can be used not only for your travel photos, but also for your favorite pictures.

**Materials**
Paper stencil works
Cardboard
Polyurethane board;
   sample size: 11.8 in x
   9 in (30 cm x 23 cm)
Acrylic sheet; sample size:
   10.2 in x 7 in
   (26 cm x 18 cm)
Spray glue
Craft knife
Cutting mat

## Steps

1

First, cut out a picture frame from the polyurethane board. Line three sides of the frame with double-sided tape, leaving one side open for sliding in images.

2

Attach the paper stencils on the cardboard with strong spray glue.

3

Stick the cardboard made in step 2 on the front of the polyurethane frame. Fold the edges inside and cut off the excessive parts.

4

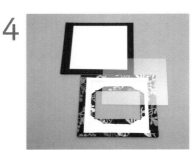

To finish, stick together the cardboard and the surface of the frame. Paste a photo on an acrylic sheet and insert it through the opening of the middle board.

# Lamp Stand

The memories of my travels shine dimly as I close my eyes to dream.

## Materials

Paper stencil works

Fiber craft paper for the light; sample size: 3 sheets of 5.5 in x 26.8 in (14 cm x 68 cm) and 2 sheets of 2.8 in x 26.8 in (7 cm x 68 cm)

Spray glue

Socket

Electric wire

Light bulb

Ruler

Craft knife

Cutting mat

Wooden stand

1

Fold the heat-resistant fiber craft paper into four parts for the light, leaving a margin to be used as the seam.

2

This lamp becomes three dimensional if you pile up square prisms. Make eight slits on each side of the prism to insert the parts.

3

Attach the paper stencils on the prisms to make the silhouette. Cut a slit with a craft knife where the stencils and the slits overlap.

4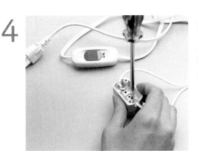

Assemble the lamp. First, attach the tip of the electric wire to the socket with a screwdriver.

5

Install the socket onto the wooden stand. Verify the center, and screw in the wooden screws vertically.

6

To finish the lamp, install a light bulb in the socket. Cover it with the shade on which you pasted your paper stencils.

*Caution: To prevent a fire incident, use heat-resistant fiber craft paper.*

# Note from the Author

I was fifteen years old on a spring day when
I first traveled abroad with my grandmother. Back
then, I could not imagine that I would live by
means of my artistic expression through creating
decorative paper stencils. After my first trip,
I continued to travel every year when I was
a student and spent all the money I saved from
my part-time job. I cannot forget those days when
I was away from Japan for several months and
came home with so many experiences.
The people who I traveled with were and are my
most important friends.

One day, I happened to cut some paper at
home and had an unusual feeling that I never had
before—a feeling that I could not explain with
words—and then I began to bring scissors with
me whenever I traveled. This is how my trip with
decorative paper stencils began, and how I began
to narrate my travel experiences through this art
form. My travelogue will continue forever as
I seek further encounters and hope to feel
nostalgic about every trip I make.

# About the Author: Kanako Yaguchi

Born in 1976, Kanako graduated from the
Department of Design at Joshibi University of Art
and Design, in Japan. As a student, she held an
exhibition, entitled "Yorokobinokatachi" ("Shapes
of Pleasure") and started activities for inventing
various shapes of decorative paper stencils, or
"kirigami." Her personal artwork is full of new
discoveries and expressions of the good old
days, which have fascinated people around the
world. Her current job involves holding individual
exhibitions while collaborating with the apparel
industry. She also does store and logo design
and holds workshops based on decorative
paper stencils. Her work has been introduced in
various media, and in 2006, she created "Saikan,"
an apparel brand that can be found in Los Angeles.

# Appendix: Decorative Paper for Paper-Stencil Making

I have created decorative paper with different colors and patterns, tracing back memories of my past travels. When you have a past memory that matches any of these paper designs, fold the paper, cut, and open. Your encounter with paper stencils will surprise you with a new discovery.

To use the paper samples, choose any design you like and cut along the dotted line. Then, cut the paper into a square or a rectangle to start making a decorative paper stencil. You can surely create a fabulous and unique piece of work.

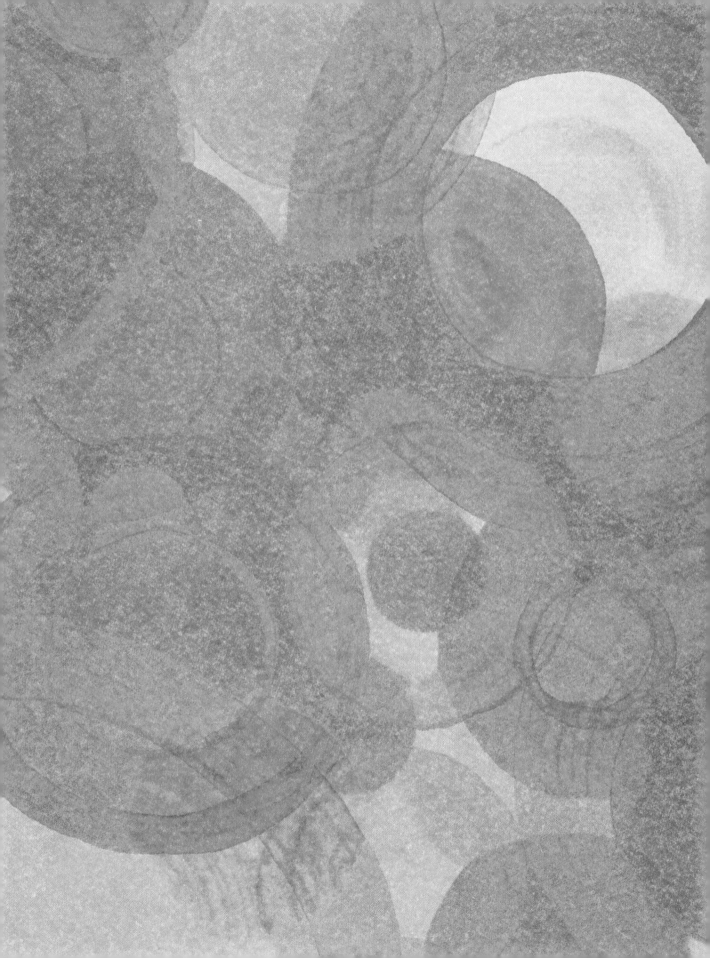

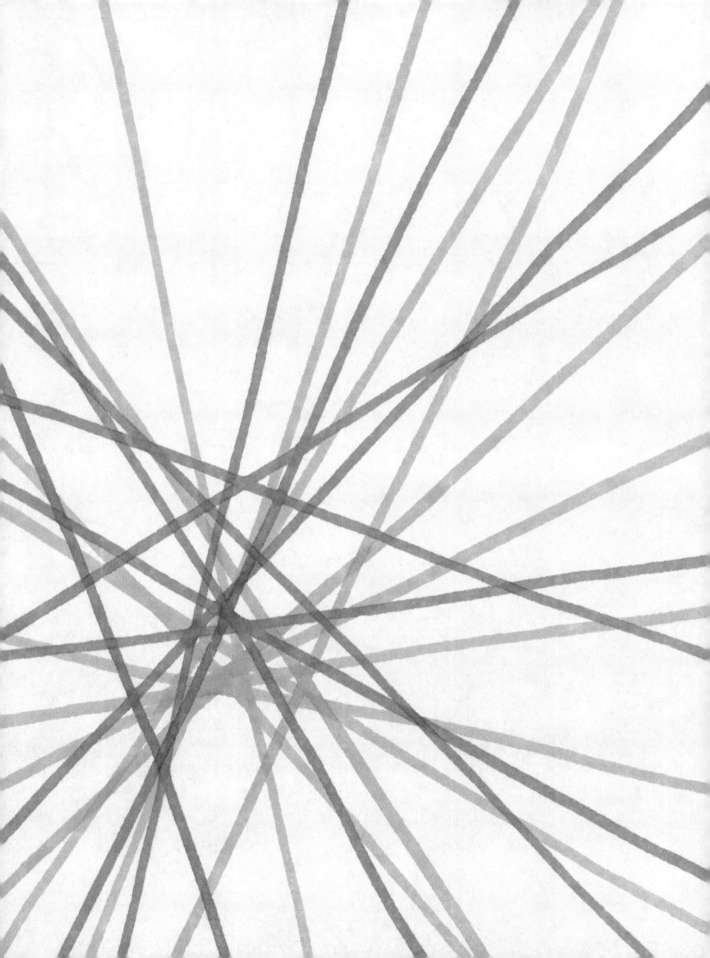

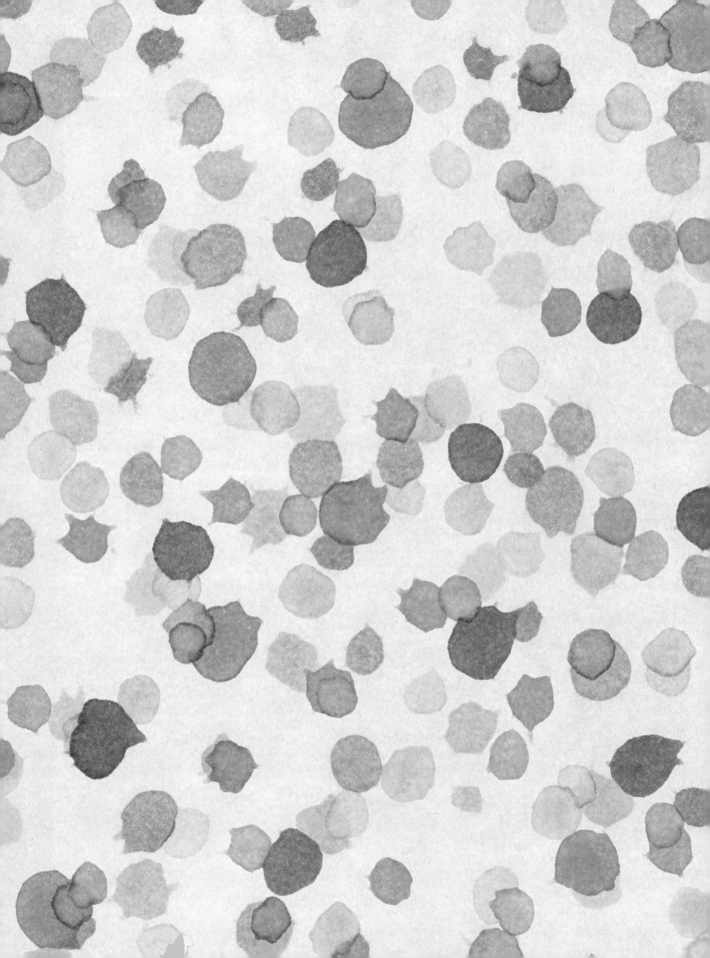